PROOF OF THE PUDDING IS IN THE MAKING OF IT

Is

Production and Operations Management

So

Si

PROOF OF THE PUDDING IS IN THE MAKING OF IT

Is
Production and Operations Management
So
Simple!

S.N. CHARY

First published in India 2017
This export edition published in 2020

ISBN 978-93-86643-05-6

Bloomsbury Publishing India Pvt. Ltd
Second Floor, LSC Building No.4
DDA Complex, Pocket C – 6 & 7, Vasant Kunj
New Delhi 110070
www.bloomsbury.com

Edited by Ruchhita Kazaria
Typeset by Manipal Digital Systems

Preface

I would like to start with salutations to my Guru and dedicate this book to Him.

The intent behind this book is to spread the wisdom and message of Production and Operations Management (POM) to a wide readership – students, busy executives from industry, and also people who imagine that they have nothing to do with management like doctors, artists and homemakers.

The book distils the POM wisdom and presents the same through common everyday examples. By the examples given in this book it is clear that POM is needed by everyone of us in all areas of life. It is an easy-to-read and fun-filled book by which a reader will get to know the gist of POM within an hour. One does not need a background in Business/Management in order to pick up this book and read.

After several decades in the management profession, I got the simplicity of POM and its applicability in various areas of life. I wanted to share this experience with a wider audience. And hence this book.

Happy reading.

Contents

Chapter 1

Proof Of The Pudding Is In The Making Of It

Production and operations management (POM) is one of the functions of overall management of an organization, like marketing management and human resource management. Somebody may get sales orders for a product or service, but it has to be made/arranged and physically delivered to the customer to the latter's satisfaction; this is done by POM. The proof of the pudding is in eating it. The pudding is made and supplied by POM. Human resources management comes after that – in order to take care of the makers, deliverers and promoters.

An athlete in a running race may know the target, the capabilities of other athletes, their previous performance history and so on; all that is of no avail until she runs and wins.

Her face may be full of determination and competition rage at the start of the competition; but, the real test comes when she runs with her feet flying from the ground and hands pushing back and forth to provide the surge to her body. She has to be flexible, nimble, quick, fast and vigilant of the other competitors; and she should not tire out. Her physio may be there to help her; but, that is after the race.

POM has always been there, even before the present day corporate world came into existence. When my great grandmother did her chores in order to deliver daily a great meal to all of us – on time three times a day – it was nothing short of any other POM.

When your great grandfather tilled the land, and took care of milk cattle, he was running an operation to keep his family well-fed and clothed. He had to not only take care of seeds and fodder but also, very importantly, mind the seasons, the timely tilling and preparing the land, timely sowing, and on time harvesting.

However, in the huge spectacle and sound of the modern industrial processing machines and the razzle-dazzle of mind-boggling and senses-satisfying services of the present-day world, we momentarily forget that the unassuming basic jobs remain the same. We just have to remove the clutter. Whether it is military operations or civilian, the simple basics are more or less similar. Timely strikes with surgical precision are as much important in military operations as in the competitive global market.

Chapter 2

Time

In general, the phrase 'Production and Operations Management' conjures up images of materials, machines and men furiously working at or with them. We also think of the amount of money that is required to have these resources. Rarely does the thought of the other resource, 'time', flash in our mind.

However, a foremost principle in managing operations is that of minimizing time. As we said, this may sound inappropriate. Is 'time' a physical resource? – one may ask. Well; Time is money. The more time we spend, the more it costs us. For instance, our own time costs us. Time is not free.

Money – in any form either as materials, machines, manpower or plain simple cash – kept for a length of time costs more money.

Moreover, remember: 'Time and tide wait for no one'. Time that is lost does not return. Time is a precious resource.

The MUST super-principle

MINIMISE:
Using
Storing and
Transporting time

Operations use resources – material and men/women. All resources – whether it is palpable 'material' like a metal sheet, a non-palpable resource like broadband for the internet, mind power like that of an engineer or a doctor diagnosing a patient – cost more when used over a longer time period. 'Minimize Using Time' means minimize the total time taken to perform any operation. Thus, the dictum is to 'Reduce Operation Times'.

Principle 1
Reduce Operation Times

Towards this goal:

1. Design parts or components of the operation so that each of the parts takes minimum possible time. Towards this:

We may use more time-efficient technology; like using Automation and Robotics for producing parts or carrying out chemical/electrochemical processes.

Utilize 'Design for Manufacturing' (DFM) and make production setups and manufacturing operations simple. This technique will be elaborated in a later chapter.

Apply 'Time Study' and 'Methods Study' towards time-efficiency in various tasks. These techniques will also be explained in a later chapter.

'Reduce':
Operations management's important mantra

2. Study the flow of work in the process. Arrange for a smooth flow in all processes.

FLOW PRINCIPLE

Note that everything is a process: An ophthalmic surgeon removing a cataract is a process; a software engineer writing a program is a process; a Drive-in restaurant taking your order and delivering the take-away food items is a process; and a telephone receptionist taking calls and transferring them is also a process. Of course, an automobile being assembled is a process, as we all know.

Arrange the components of work in such a way that the flow of work is as smooth, un-interrupted and continuous as possible. The important word is 'Flow'. Ensure a smooth flow. It is the stoppages that consume time (it is obvious), expend our mental energy in locating the stops or hitches and removing them, and in stitching the follow-up or downstream operation with the stalled operation.

An important principle, therefore, is:

Principle 2
The Flow Principle
which says
Ensure a Smooth Uninterrupted Flow

Remember, the beauty of an Assembly Line is in its uninterrupted flow. Work on the assembly line flows like a stream of water. Hence, assembly line is a phenomenally efficient management tool. It has been one of the revolutionary concepts in the history of management.

The idea behind 'balancing an assembly line' is also to ensure a uniform and unhindered flow of work, along the line from its start to a complete product, at the end of the line.

We have to learn from nature. The less a stream meanders, the smoother its flow. Zigzag flows have to be reduced as much as possible.

While the concept of assembly line is widely known for its extraordinary utility in mass production like in the assembling of components to make an automobile, the concept's application may also be found in a sensitive area such as surgery. For instance, in Moscow, patients for cataract surgery are lined up on stretchers on a conveyor belt, one after another for the surgical procedures. Since much of the procedure is standardized, the surgeries can be done by a small group of ophthalmic surgeons, anesthetists and specialized supporting nursing staff, in a manner akin to a mass production line.

1. The nurse stationed outside the Operation Theatre (OT) checks the records of the patient.
2. Upon her nod, the second nurse cleans and swabs the eye to be operated with a disinfectant. She places a clean cover over that eye, with only the eye as visible.
3. After this is done, she signals the doctor inside the OT who pulls the stretcher in and puts anaesthetizing drops into that eye. A few minutes later, when the anesthetic kicks in, he immobilizes the eye with clamps and signals the next doctor (ophthalmic surgeon).
4. The ophthalmic surgeon makes an incision into the eye in order to lift the cornea. She signals the next work station.
5. Another eye surgeon widens the incision and removes the cataract (clouded lens).
6. The next ophthalmic surgeon (the senior surgeon) has to be ready by then. He skillfully inserts the already specified artificial lens into the vacant space and closes the cornea. He checks whether the overall surgery has been done well.
7. The patient is now moved out of OT, but is made to relax on the stretcher for ten minutes. After this, the operated eye is disinfected again by a nurse outside. Thereafter, he can get up and go home.

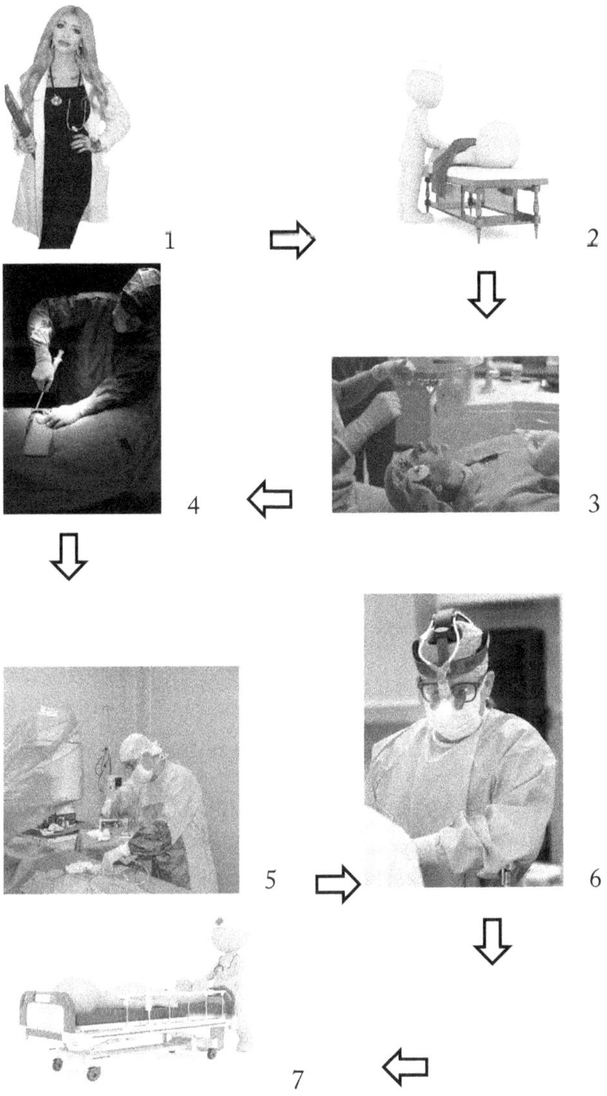

FIG. 1: Cataract Surgery on an Assembly Line

If a complication should occur – it is rare to so happen – during such assembly line surgery, the patient's operating table is quickly pulled out of the assembly line to an adjoining area where he is given special attention.

One can even think of performing surgeries on the human heart in a similar fashion by a group of surgeons, supporting junior doctors and nurses. Sounds heartless; but it is not so. It would only help reduce the costs, making best medical treatment more affordable to the suffering patients.

In a five-star hotel's restaurant, the orders too, flow in a smooth fashion from the bearer taking the order, to the item being made, garnished and presented in the dish, to its placement onto the guest's table. There has to be no confusion; no steps left out; and delivered in a standard time interval from the time it was ordered. Smooth flow of work is essential to maintaining the appearance, aesthetics, fragrance, taste, texture, temperature and the timeliness of the dish being served. Therefore, whether it is the manufacturing industry or a hospital or a hotel, an important operations management principle to remember is The Flow Principle.

Note the parallels in other domains:

The writing of an author should flow.
The oratory of a social and/or political leader should flow.
The individual frames in a movie or the scenes in a theatrical presentation should flow or be seamless.

Flow is one of Nature's properties (characteristics). Let us follow her and use her principles. You may also notice this is the reason why materials should 'flow' into the operations facility (or factory), within the factory and then out of the facility.

Inventories comprise mostly of the material that has stopped inside the operations facility. Stocking is the same as building stoppages. Why would you want to build stoppages?

We were going against the Nature's nature. Until some wise men like Henry Ford in the early twentieth century and over half a century later Toyota – a Japanese auto-maker – had a partial realization of the Nature's ways. As we understood the Nature better, the better we got in designing our operations systems.

Chapter 3

Rhythm

RHYTHM PRINCIPLE

Rhythm is another of nature's principles. It follows from the Flow principle. Rhythm depends on flow. Rhythm could even be an interrupted flow, but one that occurs at periodic intervals.

Nature's seasons are an example of rhythm. Leaves start falling during a certain period and leave the trees bare for the winter to arrive and drop its snow onto the branches. When spring arrives, the branches magically start turning green. Waves that wash the shores of an ocean also have a rhythm.

Likewise, smooth and efficient operations have a rhythm. Therefore, one more operations management principle – borrowed from Mother Nature – is:

Principle 3
The Rhythm Principle:
Establish or Restore the Rhythm of the Operations

In automobile assembly, there is a rhythm of the operations. The 'cycle time' of the assembly line is established before the work on the line starts. In any continuous and mass operations system, the rhythm or beat or cycle time is an important part of its design. In fact, the rhythm is an important objective of a production/operations system.

In a mass production or continuous system, the 'cycle time' – which is the rhythm – determines the output per unit time. In a process, the achievement of the cycle time is a main objective. The efficiency of a process depends heavily upon the cycle time. All the tasks in the process are then 'balanced' around that cycle time.

Balancing the Assembly Line

If the work-time at one work-station in an assembly line is considerably lower to that at the next work-station, the work would pile up at the latter station, which is not advisable. Moreover, it puts continuous work pressure on station two. It demoralizes the person at station two. Person at station two may feel cheated.

Also, in some cases, like the eye surgery example given earlier, (i) It is essential from a hygiene point of view that the patient is not exposed for a long time (ii) The main eye surgeon – a critical person – should get a short respite. The surgeon should not tire out. Therefore, for various reasons, attempt is made to 'balance' work at all the work-stations on the line; the work at all stations takes more or less the same time. This time is called the 'cycle time' and the latter sets the pace at which the output is obtained from the line.

It is obvious that in an assembly line, we do not want to back track the work (For instance – The patient in the eye surgery case). The line moves forward. A stream of water if it gets obstructed and accumulated, it tends to putrefy.

Batch Process and Rhythm

Even if it is a batch process, the frequency with which a batch is produced – called as batch time – determines the efficiency of that process. For instance, the production of Aluminum metal from Bauxite ore by the electrochemical process is a batch process. The efficiency of the production of the metal depends largely upon the 'batch time' of this process carried out in a large electrochemical cell.

FIG. 2: Electrolytic Cells for Producing Aluminum from Bauxite

A process in good control produces every completed batch at the same periodic interval.

When batches of different products may be produced on the same equipment, these are to be produced rhythmically – like the different notes of a *raaga* follow each other systematically. For instance, in a garment factory, on a particular equipment if the shirt collars are to be stitched for sizes 'small', 'medium', 'large' and 'extra-large', it will be an efficient operation, if the same sequence or rhythm is followed batch after batch of the shirts.

Which 'size' or style of collar is to be followed by which other size or style is dependent on the technical aspects. It need not start with the 'small' and end with 'extra-large'. However, once a sequence (or rhythm) is decided, it may be maintained for some time to come. In each rhythmic pulse, how many 'small' or other sizes are to be produced, would depend upon the overall requirement or demand for that size. It is easy to understand that nobody wants to produce a large lot of production and wait for customer orders to deplete that said stock. That would involve carrying much inventory. Smaller lots – tending towards single unit production – would be preferred.

But, there are costs associated with making frequent changes in the production sequence: The machines, the tools, the workplace, the materials handling system to move the raw and finished goods and the workforce may have to be rearranged for every change in the pattern of sequence. For the garment factory example, the changeover would be more acutely felt if the change was from one style of garment to another; like from shirt to a *kurti* (long Indian shirt for women). People lump these costs under the sub-head of 'set-up costs'. The latter could be substantial.

Optimal or Economic Batch Quantities

Therefore, one desires a 'golden mean' between not carrying too many items and not incurring considerable set-up costs. This is called 'Economic Batch Quantity' (EBQ) of production or 'Economic Order Quantity' (EOQ).

$$EBQ = \sqrt{\{2C_p\, A\, p/C_c\, (p - r)\}}$$

Where, C_p is Cost of setup in Rs per setup, A is annual demand of the item in numbers, C_c is cost of carrying the item in inventory Rs. per unit per year, p and r are the production and consumption rates respectively of the item in numbers per day.

Suppose then that there are four sizes of shirts to be made on a set of equipment. Suppose for all the sizes of shirts, the C_p, A, C_c, p and r are Rs. 1,000 per setup, 18,000 numbers per annum, Rs. 300 per year per shirt, and 200 numbers and 50 numbers per day.

$$EBQ = \sqrt{\{2000 \times 18000 \times 200/300\ (200 - 50)\}} = 400$$

This is the optimal batch quantity; which is to say that the setup is changed (for a different size) every two days, for this example. That is the 'rhythm' of this operation.

Similarly, for purchases the optimal quantity or economic order quantity (EOQ) is given by:

$$EOQ = \sqrt{\{2C_p A / C_c\}}$$

This EOQ is the 'rhythm' for the purchases of the item.

More than the formulae, one should look at the concepts behind them.

Is Single Unit Production Possible?

We notice that the EBQ shrinks to a smaller and smaller quantity as we reduce the set-up costs. When a change-over can be done very quickly – almost instantaneously and therefore at a negligible cost – we can afford to produce one single unit of item at a time. So, we would not have to carry any raw material or work-in-progress inventory other than that one unit of item, in the production system.

> **Sub-principle:**
> ***When set-up time and cost shrinks the economically viable batch size of an operation reduces.***
> **Therefore,**
> **Reduce the Set-up Time.**

In the previous chapter, it was emphasized that the 'operation time' was to be reduced. Setting up is also an operation. Reduction in its time – if it is accompanied by reduction in costs, since time is money – has a catalytic effect on the operations. It sets up a faster 'beat' or 'rhythm' to the entire system of operations.

Fast Beat and Smooth Flow

This concept of quick changeovers was powerfully pioneered by Toyota Production System, over four decades ago. Quick and, therefore, smooth changeovers are in line with the Flow principle.

Toyota Production System

Toyota Production System made it possible to have almost no inventories of work-in-process (WIP) items. This was possible due to a sharp reduction in changeover times and costs.

Single minute exchange of dies (SMED) is one such rapid changeover system. Toyota further improved to 'one touch' changeovers. The Toyota system questioned the very existence of set up times and set up costs, which the world had taken for granted.

Finished Goods and Raw Materials inventories also got radically reduced as a consequence. Cutting down WIP was like shedding weight around one's middle; or like cutting out the clutter from the office desk. The effect was electrifying!

More on Toyota will follow in the later pages. Organizations – private sector and public sector – and individuals have to get into rhythm. They have got to shed weight and should be able to get into faster beat when required. Leave aside competitiveness, mere viability is a problem if they cannot do so.

Chapter 4

Agility

AGILITY ADVANTAGE

Any rhythm needs agility. If a system has to find rhythm and function well under varying circumstances, i.e. unexpected variations in circumstances, it needs to be agile. Without agility, rhythm is likely to break.

A system of operations that can take a faster beat has to have more flexibility. A dancer, who has to dance to a quick beat and to varying beats, has to be supple. S/he has to attempt to shed weight, be 'lean' and be nimble. Similarly, in our attempt to make the beat of the production system faster, we prepare the operations to be 'leaner' than before and more flexible than before.

It is not that a not-so-lean person cannot dance. But, it would be preferable, if the bulk was to be reduced substantially.

Is this Rhythm principle true mostly for 'manufacturing' operations? No. It is true for all operations – whether in the manufacturing sector or in the service sector. For example, a relatively good restaurant's kitchen has a rhythm. Such a kitchen is supple. It is nimble so as to meet the variations in an order or variations on the customer's table quickly.

This brings us to the principle of 'agility'.

Principle 4
The Agility Principle:
Make Operations Agile

Operations Strategy: Quickness to Respond

In nature, the agile creatures survive better, compete better and respond to the changed circumstances lightning quickly. Lion, tiger, cheetah and similar cats hunt animals much bigger than their own size. This is possible because they are nimble and swift in their attack. Being agile also lends greater speed and swiftness to them. They can accelerate and attain high speeds within an instant or two; they can also decelerate, come to a halt and reverse the direction in an instant. Same is also true of operations. Agile operations compete better. Agile organizations are there much before the others arrive on the market scene. Importantly, they help the organization serve its customers or target groups better.

Health services in a country, if they are agile, would be much better able to take on sudden patient load due to unforeseen natural calamities or due to new disease vectors. An agile airline would be better able to handle passenger traffic in new sectors; also, uncertain traffic situations due to bad weather or other unforeseen circumstances could be handled with efficiency and care towards the passengers.

Fire department of any city has to be agile. It should be nimble so as to quickly reach the accident spot, save the lives of people and douse the fire.

How to enhance agility?

What is being 'agile'? What is being 'lean'? When we say that an organization is 'agile' what do we mean by it? Is it necessary that organizations be 'lean' in order to be 'agile'?

Agility is the ability to respond quickly and easily to changed or unusual circumstances. Lean is like being slim; agility is like being athletic. Most athletes are slim but not all slim people are athletic. However, slim persons are more likely to be athletic than stocky persons. The starting point of athleticism is slimming down.

Shedding weight helps to make a person more nimble; but, bulk is only one of the factors – although an important factor. Similarly, shedding weight in an organization i.e. shedding inventories, over-production, over-staffing, excess capital investment in infrastructure and equipment is an important factor that could make the organization more agile.

Principle 5:
Shed Weight.
Shedding weight helps in making an organization more agile

Leanness – rather the lack of it – depends on factors other than the obvious weight or bulk in the organization. Somebody is lean, when there is nothing excess in his/her body than what is needed. In an operation, all 'non-value adding' work has to be eliminated. By 'value' we mean 'value to the customer'.

Blind to the flab?

In the previous paragraph, the obvious 'non-value adding' factors had been identified – like inventories, over-production and so on. But in a number of cases, some 'flab' i.e. non-value adding tasks are justified as 'essential' non-value adding tasks. 'Under the given system of work' or 'under the prevailing technology' or 'under the prevailing business environment', that non-value adding task is perceived to be essential.

'Taking it for granted' or self-deception is a huge 'flab' in most organizations. Waits or idle times, transport or movement of material and men, certain fraction of defects or defective units are some of the things that are taken for granted. These constitute a sizable flab in the organization and its operations.

How to make operations agile?

Reducing the organizational fat helps hugely in making the organization i.e. its operations less lethargic. But, 'agile organization' or 'agile operations' are more than just being less lethargic. Such an organization is highly responsive in a less predictable environment or when the variability is high or the demands are dynamic. Agility is the ability to react quickly to an unpredictable environment. 'Agile' operations are one step ahead of 'Lean' operations.

Agile operations have to respond rapidly as the new circumstances present themselves. Therefore, they may involve more automation and take the support of Information Technology. Instantaneous logistics response and rapid product design changes are essential to lend agility. There has to be a highly integrated information technology communication system throughout the organization and its supply chain and other business affiliates. In fact, fluid clusters may help in the place of rigid supply chains.

Chapter 5

Punctuality

PUNCTUALITY & DISCIPLINE

Efficiencies generated due to flow & rhythm and agility to grab a customer order are welcome. But, what is in it for the customer? These organizational competitive advantages have to translate into an advantage *for the customer*. Whether you are agile or not, all that the customer wants is that *his* needs should be satisfied at a time he wants; or at a time you have agreed to provide those services/products to him. Therefore, punctually sticking to promised schedules of delivery (of products and/or services) is a vital competitive operations strategy.

Scheduling is, hence, very important. Whether in a manufacturing job shop, a restaurant or in a hospital's out-patient department, the jobs and guests/patients have to be scheduled in such a way that the customers/ guests/patients are served by the expected time. How does an organization find out the particular time (or time schedule) to promise to the customer – a time/schedule by/at which it can deliver?

PERT/CPM charts

PERT/CPM chart is useful. It analyzes the web of inter-connected tasks and computes the time by which the service/product can be delivered. The chart is a pictorial representation of the sequence in which the tasks can follow each other; the time estimates of the individual tasks are also shown. Very simple arithmetical calculations determine that a few tasks are 'critical' to completing the delivery on time; these have to be closely monitored.

We will illustrate this using a household project that is familiar to most parents of a young child. Young Chintu has to be taken to the school bus early in the morning; Chintu's Mom is being helped by a maid. Fig. 3 is a PERT/CPM diagram for that project; it shows the tasks (called 'activities') in the usual sequence. Each arrow depicts the task with its time estimate.

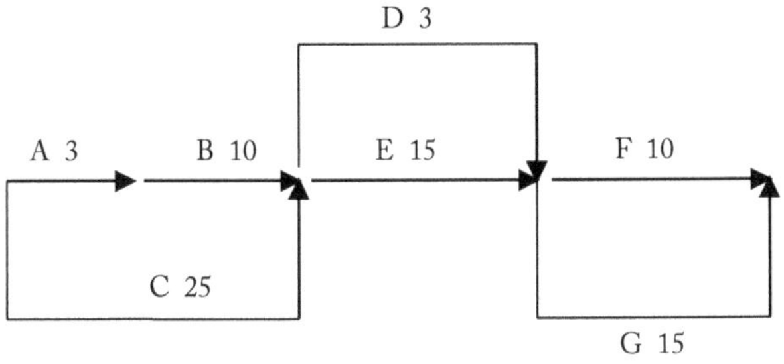

A = Mom brushes	B = Mom makes tea
C = Chintu brush & toilet	D = Mom has tea
E = Chintu has milk	F = Chintu dresses up
G = Mom dresses up	

FIG. 3: PERT/CPM Chart for Project 'Sending Chintu to School-bus'

We see that the entire process of getting up and being ready to go to school takes fifty-five minutes ('activities' C, E and G are 'critical' and take twenty-five, fifteen and fifteen minutes respectively). The chart also informs us that if 'Chintu brushing and going to toilet', 'Chintu drinking milk' and

'Mom dressing up' can be reduced in time, then Chintu will be ready earlier with lesser tension of missing the school bus. Chintu's activities can be made faster if additional resources are made available like say his Dad hurrying him up with brushing and drinking milk. Of course, Mom dressing up faster will also help to some extent.

We see that these PERT/CPM charts are of great help in monitoring a project (in this case: the project of sending Chintu up to the school-bus), deciding on which tasks to focus on, deciding on resources to be made available and so on. In several projects (e.g. power generation, railway laying, new product launch), the number of activities and resources could be very large. However, computer programs are readily available that help management decision-making.

Principle 6: Punctuality & Discipline
Be Punctual. Deliver as Promised or Expected.
It builds great credibility with the customer and discipline and confidence within the organization itself.

Gantt chart

In many cases, simpler bar charts showing the planned schedule and also depicting the extent of completion (on a particular day) are useful. 'Gantt chart' is one such chart.

Prioritization of jobs

If the process of manufacturing or service-providing involves a job going through several machine centers or a customer going through several stages of service, certain 'sequencing rules' help in putting them through faster. Few examples of these 'order dispatching rules' are:

- Johnson's rule
- *Shortest operation time* next
- *Minimum slack per operation* next (slack = time until due date less total processing time remaining divided by number of operations left)
- *Earliest due date job* next

Using 'shortest operation time' next rule if we allow a houseful of people in a single bathroom in the morning, the persons with a need to just brush may all get their job done. But those with a need to bathe – needing longer time – may remain at the back of the queue. Thus, each sequencing rule has its boons and banes.

We may have to use one rule first and then truncate it and use another prioritization rule, to take care of the remaining persons or jobs. For instance, after the brushing, use the 'Earliest due time' rule to ensure that each person completes his/her chores by the time he/she is supposed to leave for work. The whole idea behind 'scheduling' of operations is to deliver goods/services to the customers timely.

Chapter 6

Space

A consideration of paramount importance

Space, in connection to operations, has two different aspects: Location and Arrangement.

Location

While buying real estate, we consider the location of estate carefully. In fact, many estate consultants will tell you that the valuation is about three aspects: '*Location*', '*Location*' and '*Location*'. In operations, it is no different; perhaps it is a shade more important.

For different kinds of operations, different aspects or purposes of location may be crucially important. For instance:

- **Reach**: A fire station has to be located in a central place from where the fire equipment can rapidly reach all parts of the town. (Critical question in choosing the location: Can help from the fire station reach the disaster site quickly?)
- **Accessibility and Quietude**: Whereas a hospital should be easily reachable, but preferably located in a quiet and secluded area such as the outskirts of the town; it need not be in the centre of the town. (Critical question in choosing the location for a hospital: Will the hospital be easily accessible to the people in need; will it be located in a quiet area?)

- **Coverage**: In rural areas of India, a primary or secondary school may be so located that it covers maximum population within a radius of approximately five kilometers. (Critical question in choosing the location: Will it serve a large number of school-going children?)
- **Resources availability**: In the rural school location decision, another important question is: where would the qualified teachers be willing to work? (Critical question: Will the children get any/proper teachers to teach them?)
- **Minimize potential hazard**: A factory dealing with potentially hazardous chemicals should be located far from densely populated areas. (Critical question: Is it located so as to minimize any hazards to the people?)

What we see from the above is that the considerations of the customers are important. In locating a service business, one looks at the nature and volume/size of clientele. If my restaurant is upscale, it goes without saying that it should be located in an upscale locality of the town/city. If it was to be a fast-selling *dosa-idli-puri-bhaji* outlet, it should preferably be located in a very busy area of the town or near business offices, where people would come out in large numbers, for a quick bite.

The above examples were for relatively small facilities; the location decisions of large businesses even for MNC's are similar, but they may start the search from Country, to State/ Province within that country, narrowing down to a city/ town in that State. In addition to the potential or existing market size and market complexion and competition, other factors may be equally or more important there:

- Politics/Political stability/Viability in that political environment

- Government policies, taxes, subsidies, incentives and so on
- Social acceptance (e.g. 'Foreigners Go Home' type of movements or sentiment?)
- Availability of required technological infrastructure and technical skills

Thus, starting with the market's size and its nature, resource availability including technical skills, availability of needed infrastructure, one checks the political and social environment in which the business will have to function. Economics and cost/profit computations can be done in detail after the critical conditions are alright. A good location decision is crucial to the success of the operation: be it a public facility or a business/industry. Location is a strategic decision. Not just for 'operations', but also for locating and committing to a 'market', much prudence has to go in.

Principle 7:
Thoughtful Commitment

Location decision is like marriage.
Much prudence has to go into it,
while committing to it.

During the 1970's, a large iron-ore mining and concentrating facility was established in the coastal area of India, with a committed market, limited to one country. Just after the start of the company, the latter country had a huge political upheaval and the mining company's market just vanished. There were few takers for the product (concentrated ore) it produced and the product had to be sold at throw-away prices in the International market.

Complementarities

Location is not always a single location decision. A business or public service may have several facilities to be located in such a way that they complement each other or boost each other. It is possible that they may be the different components of the supply chain. Complementarities are important in deciding in location/s.

Arrangement of Space i.e. Layout

Once the operational facility is located, the next task is to make certain that it does what it is intended to do, which is:

Be effective: provide the intended/promised service;

Be efficient: provide it at competitive cost/price.

Be safe: ensure safety while providing the service

Spatial arrangement of the processes – also called 'layout', contributes substantially towards the above three goals.

Process Layout

If a large variety of products are to be produced or services provided, by making use of a limited variety of operations, it makes sense to group together one kind of equipment or service operators. All cutting machines together in one space, all grinding machines together in another, all painting machines in a third space, and so on. All physicians in one unit, all cardiologists in another unit, urologists in a third unit, all pathological tests in another and so on. This is called a 'Process Layout' i.e. a layout according to the specialized process.

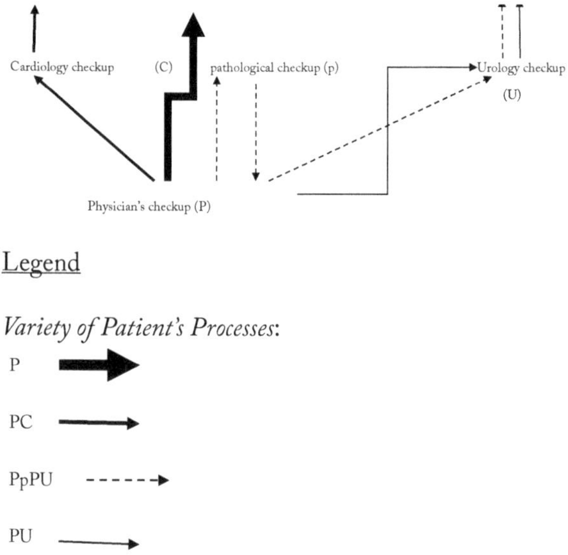

FIG. 4: Process Layout for a Hospital

As the above figure shows, each patient may require different flows between the various medical specialties in the hospital. There could be a large variety (although the figure shows only four types of flow).

With such an arrangement, the various specialists – whose daily fees are very expensive – are utilized to the maximum. The equipment in these units is expensive; its utilization is also maximized.

You, as a patient, know that the problem with this arrangement is that on some days certain operations could make you wait for hours. You may have come just for a simple blood test; but you may have to wait for a long time just to give the sample of blood.

With respect to physical goods, some orders are filled in quickly; some have to wait for long. There is an element of unpredictability with regard to the completion times. The work-in-process inventories can be large at times. A 'process layout' may be efficient for the organization, making good use of the resources of the units. But, it may not be 'customer friendly'. So, does it provide the service that was intended/promised? Also, remember: what is not 'customer friendly' now is not 'organization friendly' in the longer term.

Keep customers happy through Sequencing rules or Dispatch rules

In order to ensure that the short and urgent jobs (e.g. blood test for sugar level in diabetics) are not made to wait for long, in industries we may use 'sequencing rules' such as 'Shortest Operation Time first (SOT)' giving preference to small operation time jobs. We read about these 'sequencing rules' in the previous chapter.

Principle 8: Keep it Simple and Safe.
Basics of Layout:
Ease, Economy and Safety

Economy in Movements

A 'cost' in the Process Layout is the movement of materials (in manufacturing) and of people (customers in service operations). We have to minimize the total *Load × Distance* between all the pairs of processing units or departments for all the products. In the previous figure, 'Load' means the number of patients in a day

Suppose on an average day, 200 patients come to the Physicians, a hundred are referred to the Pathology Lab, thirty to the Cardiology and fifty to the Urology. There arc no other referrals from one department to any other department. If the distance between the pairs of departments is: Pp: 0.1 Km, PC: 0.2 Km, PU: 0.3 Km, then,

Cost = *Load* × *Distance* = 100 × 0.1 + 30 × 0.2 + 50 × 0.3 = 31 men Km.

By rearranging, for instance, U in the place of C and vice versa, would the 'cost' be lowered? Indeed! It would be: 100 × 0.1 + 50 × 0.2 + 30 × 0.3 = 29 men Km. So, rearrange.

This was common sense. But, since hundreds of different jobs have to move through a factory 'layout', industries take the help of algorithms that minimize the total *Load* × *Distance* between all the pairs of processing units or departments for all the products. The distances are taken as center to center distances between a pair of departments. Loads are the number of times materials are moved between a pair of departments.

CRAFT

There are computer programs such as CRAFT (Computerized Relative Allocation of Facilities Technique) that minimize the cost that was mentioned above. It is particularly useful when several products involve several different sequences, with different loads through several departments. Per load per unit distance cost of material handling between departments 1 & 2 may be quite different from that for departments 1 & 3. Such differences also are taken into consideration in CRAFT. Various different spatial arrangements of the departments are checked for the 'cost'; an arrangement that offers lowest cost is accepted.

Ensuring safety

Some software programs like CORELAP and ALDEP ensure that the departments that should not be near – for safety or other reasons – are not placed near each other;

those that should be near are placed as near as possible. The more qualitative 'proximity relationships' between pairs of departments is respected through such programs. 'Proximity relationships' replace the earlier *Load × Distance* computations.

Product Layout or Line Layout

An 'assembly line' is a Line layout or Product layout. Assembly line was discussed in Chapter 2. The big advantage is the 'flow' characteristic of the Line layout. A line layout eliminates the need for huge inter-departmental movements that characterize the process layout. That is a big 'waste' associated with the latter.

But, the disadvantage with a line layout may be the duplication of equipment; the capital costs could, therefore, be high. Moreover, a line is set for a particular product; for making a changeover to a different product, the whole line may have to be stopped and reset. Line allows 'flow', but its 'flexibility' or ability to produce varied products could be low.

Cellular Manufacturing

In order to have both the benefits – flow and flexibility, we may have short 'lines' in the place of work centers of a process layout. Components that require similar machines and similar setups are grouped together – called a 'family' of parts. They run through a variety of machines arranged in a center called 'cell'. Hence the name "Cellular Manufacturing". This arrangement is also called 'Group Technology (GT)'. The various components that can be manufactured in a cell can be jointly visualized as a 'composite component'. On the shop floor, there are many such 'cells' catering to different composite components. Movement between cells is discouraged.

GT is limited by its concern only to the internal spatial arrangement. However, operations depend considerably on external arrangements as well. What the suppliers/vendors do equally impacts the effectiveness and efficiency of the delivery of the product/service to the customer.

Moreover, GT does not do away with producing in 'batches'. Since each product needs a specific setup of a machine, and since a setup may take a considerable time, any product is produced in large numbers i.e. in a batch in order to do justice to the time lost in setting up. Due to this batch production, some number of inventories – raw material, WIP and finished goods – will always be there.

Toyota Production System and Layouts

We have referred to Toyota Motor Company earlier. It was a pioneer in introducing a 'single unit production' on a line. Unless the setup times for equipment are really low – single minute or even 'one-touch', meeting market needs of a variety of products on single unit basis is not possible. Toyota precisely achieved such drastic reduction in setup times, making it possible to reap advantages of both; the Process and the Line layouts. Toyota got rid of the main impediment – the 'Batch production' which is a characteristic of production in a Process layout. The size of the batch got hammered, to almost a single unit. This made it possible to have product variety while maintaining a continuous production. Toyota Production System has many radical and advantageous aspects to it. We shall visit another such aspect in Chapter 9.

Chapter 7

Material Resources – Choice

Materials are important in the production of goods and services. It is said that in a manufacturing industry, on an average 65 per cent of the cost of production of the physical goods, is that of the materials. This means that if we manage the materials well, we would manage a huge chunk of the cost of production. This is true of all operations including the service operations.

Product Design

Therefore, it goes without saying that we should design a product with the view that the usage of materials; certainly the expensive materials – is minimal. It all begins with the design of the product. By 'product', we also mean a 'service product'.

Value Analysis

Value Engineering or Value Analysis is a systematic search for substitute materials or about reducing the amount of the expensive material in a product. We analyze in details about the 'value' functional and/or esteem – of the components and 'brainstorm', coming up with substitutes that retain the same 'value' or 'worth' but cost less. Particularly those components of the product are brainstormed, whose 'cost to worth' ratio is significantly high.

Principle 9:
Simple Substitutes
***Akal Chalao, Paisa Bachao* (Use your Wits, Save your Money)**
***Kam Daam, Wohi Kaam* (Less Expense, Same Function)**

Life Cycle Cost

'Product Design' is the mother and grandmother of all things that follow:

- Manufacturing cost (or Operations cost in service organizations) for the organization
- Quality costs for the organization
- Operating cost for the customer
- Maintenance cost for the customer
- Depreciation cost for the customer
- Environmental costs (after the disposal of the remnants of the product) for the customer and the society

All of the above costs put together over the entire lifetime (and disposal thereafter) are called the 'Life Cycle cost'.

It is said that the early childhood between zero to five years is what shapes our persona. Similarly, it is for the inanimate products. A high proportion of a product's life cycle cost – Westinghouse Company said 75 per cent – is 'locked in' or committed at the early stages of its design. Therefore, it is vital to consider life-cycle costs right at the stage when product/service design is getting conceptualized.

Principle 10: Right Conceptualization.
Conceptualize right, for a future so bright.

Design of a Service Product defines the Organization's Strategy

For a service company, the service design, i.e. the service product it offers, defines the very business of that organization. It is of long time strategic importance, which is much more important than the life cycle costs. A manufacturing company can upgrade its product; but can a 'budget hotel' change its image to a high priced hi-fi hotel that easily?

Have Quality 'designed into' the Product

Reverting back to the design of a physical product, it may be noted that quality can be 'designed into' the product. It is easy to understand that quality characteristics such as reliability can be enhanced by having redundancy or by improving the weakest component. 'User-friendliness' is another quality characteristic that can be designed into the product by various means: For instance, simplify the tasks for the user. Use principles of 'Poka Yoke' i.e. preventing incorrect use (e.g. the everyday pen-drive). Use principles of 'standardization' so that the user is already familiar with the operation of the product.

Design for Manufacture (DFM)

The manufacturing costs can be lowered by using the principles of 'Design for Manufacture (DFM)'. Have such a design of the product that will be easier to manufacture, and quicker and less expensive to produce.

Actions to be taken are simple:

- Minimize the number of parts.
- Use standard/catalogue components.
- Slight modifications in the design can make fabrication and/or assembling much easier. For instance, a 'snap fit' is far easier than fitting with nuts and bolts.

- Make use of 'modules' where possible.
- Use 'Poka Yoke' or fool-proofing.

There can be various other considerations during product design, as was mentioned while describing 'Life cycle cost', like:

- Design for easy maintenance
- Design for ecologically safe disposal (of the product after it serves its complete utility)

Design for Excellence (DFX)

Although this comment comes at the end of this chapter, always remember that a product is made for providing the kind and extent of service desired by the customers. Therefore, it is always 'Design for the Customer's Requirements'.

However, while keeping this paramount interest in consideration, the aspects of quality, material cost, and ease of procuring, ease of manufacturing/operation and of maintenance, people's safety, and environmentally safe disposal when the product's life is over should also enter while designing a product. We may say, it is Design for Excellence (DFX).

Chapter 8

Materials: Get It Done by Others

Supply Chain Management & Outsourcing

Everything need not be made by us. Barring the essential items – those in which only we have the expertise, those that involve a trade or technological secret – many components (sometimes an entire item) of a product or service can be got done by others. These are the days of global team-work.

For instance, in an automobile, only the engine – what we may consider as our core expertise – may be manufactured by us. Rest of the components, including the body, can be outsourced. It makes sense, because different manufacturers may be better – cost-wise and quality-wise – at making particular parts. They may be specialized and may be handling a large volume driving their costs down. In fact, outsourcing can free up time for us to think over some of the other more crucial decisions.

> **Principle 11: Outsource**
> **Concentrate on Your Core Strengths.**
> **Get the Rest of it Done by Others.**

There are various ways of outsourcing the production process.

1. Outsource certain components. Like, if we want to make Biryani at home for a large gathering, we may buy cleaned and cut vegetables and meat from the shop.

2. Outsource assembling of final product. Our lady of the house would give the correct recipe and supply all the ingredients – daal, rice, meat pieces, vegetables, masalas (spices) – in the right quantities along with instructions for cooking to an outside caterer. The latter would put all the ingredients together, cook and send the Biryani along with his personnel who would serve to all the guests at the function.
3. Outsource the entire production. Our lady may just concentrate on her major task of receiving the guests, making polite conversation, taking care of their comfort, and so on while the Biryani making (including procuring ingredients) and serving is totally the function of the caterer.

Contract Manufacturing

The last (third) option mentioned above is called 'Contract Manufacturing'. Many companies do that. Some cosmetic multinational giants like Amway, Avon and Yardley rely on Contract Manufacturers who would do the entire production job including procuring component materials, manufacturing and then shipping the finished items to various customers of these cosmetic companies as per their specific instructions. Avon alongside others, concentrate on marketing and product development. Many Indian pharmaceutical companies are contract manufacturers for MNC pharmaceutical giants.

Research and Development (R&D), Business Research and Analysis, Personnel functions, IT and Data Processing are some of the services that are outsourced in a big way these days.

Reliable Suppliers

Since there is outsourcing on a global basis, it has become essential for the main company to stick to few, but reliable suppliers. Too many and ever-changing suppliers could lead to uncertainty and loss of control over the operations. With competitiveness of global standards being the need of the day, it is imperative to have close coordination between the main company and its suppliers. In fact, a supplier's supplier also can rock the boat. Hence, one needs to have control over the entire 'supply chain'. One cannot afford to have a weak link in the chain.

Commitment, trust, reliability and security are absolutely necessary between the various firms in the supply chain. A goal-alignment between partner organizations, sharing of information – regarding short range requirements, long range plans, and unanticipated problems at any of the supplier companies – and joint problem-solving are some of the highlights of such supply chains. It is akin to a close-knit family.

Principle 12:
Promote Relationships and Trust.
Supply chains and global business run on trust.

When we speak of 'Operations Management', these two words give an impression of a science that is very 'mechanical' in nature. However, the truth is that 'operations' can only be successful if supported by camaraderie, relationships and trust between the supply chain members. A fractured relationship makes the chain vulnerable to a sudden breakdown.

Chapter 9

Material Resources – Stocking?

After having made the proper choice of material resources during and after the decision on the design of the product, the next action would be to stock the needed material. In addition to the raw materials, we may have to stock intermediate goods as work-in-progress (WIP) inventory. We may also have to keep a stock of finished goods so that whenever the customers demand, it could be met immediately.

As we noted in Chapter 3, inventories constitute a large chunk of the production cost. In order to minimize this cost, managements have always been asking, 'How much stock should be maintained?' A large body of operations management literature called 'inventory control' intends to deal with this 'How much?' question.

The Economic Ordering Quantity (EOQ) and Economic Batch Quantity (EBQ) formulae, which we noted in Chapter 3, are such an attempt. Inventories have been 'controlled' by basically two systems.

1. ***Fixed Order Quantity system***: Imagine two bins having certain stock in each of them. Keep drawing from the first bin; when that bin gets empty, place an order for replenishment. Now draw from the second bin which contains enough quantity of the item to last until the ordered quantity arrives. Shift back to the first bin once the ordered material arrives.

2. ***Fixed Order Period system***: Instead of the order quantity, the order period is constant here. Like, every three months place an order for materials. The ordered quantity will be such that together with the inventory on hand it equals a notional quantity.

Both the systems, thus, involve stocking some material for average consumption during the interim period until the new ordered material arrives.

But what would happen if the consumption exceeds the average rate? There would be a risk of 'stock out' (having no material) until such time that the fresh stocks arrive. This would halt the operations midway. In order to avoid such a stoppage, we provide 'buffer stock' (also called 'safety stock') in the inventory. Depending upon our 'fear' level, we provide a higher level of these buffer stocks.

Therefore, the answer to the 'how much stock to keep' question depends upon the normal rate of usage of the material and our notion of 'safety stock', in a bid to cover any uncertainties in the material supply. And, we need to be bothered about 'how large' the stock is.

Seems logical?

No, it is not.

The time element in inventories

The paradox is:

The most important consideration in saving on inventories is NOT as to 'how much' to keep, but 'how long' to keep.

One ton of inventory (of raw materials and/or work-in-process and/or finished goods) kept for **one hour**

may cost almost as much as just

One kilogram of inventory lying for **one month**.

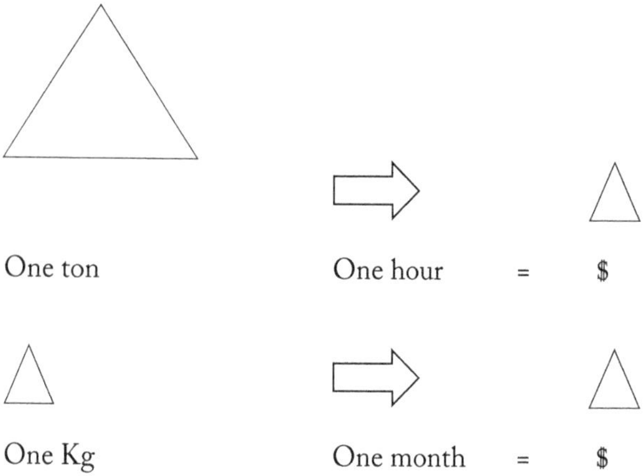

FIG. 5: 'How long?' is an important consideration

1 month has 30 × 24 = 720 hours. So, the material lies in our stores or on the shop-floor for 720 hours. Therefore, keeping 1 Kilogram for 1 month, costs in the range of stocking 1 ton for 1 hour. Not just that.

The arithmetic of costs is not as simple as 1000 × 1 versus 1 × 720. In fact,

$$1000 \times 1 < 1 \times 720$$

The longer we keep, the more would be the interest and other costs on the capital locked as raw material, work-in-process and finished goods inventory.

Also, the longer we keep the material the more would be the chances of it:

- getting spoilt/corroded
- getting damaged
- getting stolen
- needing expense on insuring it and/or maintaining it in good condition

- occupying valuable space
- incurring transport costs every time it (or a part of it) is moved
- needing space for it to be moved from stores to workplace
- getting obsolete if it gets too old, and
- all of the above necessitating supervisory effort and managerial attention.

After a long time, management may tend to overlook or forget about the items sitting in the stores. Non-moving items can become a problem sometimes.

Carrying Cost

All of the above-mentioned costs including the cost of the capital constitute the 'cost of carrying' the inventory. We had visited 'carrying costs' in the earlier pages. However, the vital point is:

The carrying cost is not necessarily proportional to the time spent and could probably get much higher in comparison to the increase in time.

Time is cost and the cost can get disproportionately larger with time.

Principle 13: Time element is extremely important in inventories

'How much?' is not as important as 'How long to keep?' Do not worry too much about 'How much' to stock? Bother a lot more about 'For how short a time' can we stock?

Stock for as little a time as possible.
If possible, don't stock at all.

Imagine, if you had a genie who would deliver the supplies to the shop–floor, exactly as required. If this is done without fail, why do you need to stock?

Just in Time

In the real world, this would require your vendors to supply the material to you just in time it is required. Such an arrangement is possible for most items; though not all. It requires an understanding between the manufacturing firm and the vendor; it requires good information sharing between the two.

In fact, the 'supply chains', which were described in the previous chapter, facilitate such understanding.

What about the stock of finished goods? Well, if your company is a supplier to another firm, you will produce the finished goods just in time they are required.

The entire production system of a firm will be 'pulled' by the demand for the firm's final product. Toyota Motor Company of Japan used such a system much before others emulated it. Hence such a production system is also called "Toyota Production System".

'Pull' instead of 'Push'

Just-in-time (JIT) or 'Toyota Production System' is a 'pull' system of production; whereas, earlier all along we were in a 'push' system. Produce an item, and push it to the next process. This creates unnecessary pressure on the processes; and generates WIP inventories (and finished goods) that are unnecessary.

An irony in the 'push' system is that 'efficiency' could sometimes be a curse, as increased efficiencies would generate more stocks of processed and semi-processed goods. Imagine two processes next to each other. Increased efficiency in the first process would cause a pile-up of work-in-process material in front of the downstream process and much annoyance.

JIT is a production system that believes in 'To everybody, according to the need'. Does it not remind us of what Mahatma Gandhi said?

Toyota Production System: Need for Super Short Set-up Times and Multi-Skilled Workers

Since production of a small Just in Time order has to be filled in super quick time, JIT system requires the set-up times of machinery to be very short. In fact, 'single touch set-ups' are useful.

Once such super short set-ups are used and small – just desired – quantities are produced, the production system could very well use Line layouts for the machinery involved. It is an effective hybrid system with single unit production or small batch production on a line layout. The workers also need to be multi-skilled in order to switch over to different kinds of operations.

If Toyota Production System is fully implemented, it leads to almost nil or minimal stocks of inventory all around. It is a simple principle of using Time discipline in operations. Discipline in the domain of Time leads to effectiveness and efficiency in the domain of Materials stocking.

Along with 'time discipline', we note that it needs a high degree of 'people coordination and cooperation'. It is about relationships between people at all levels, and relationships between organizations at all levels. Firm to vendor relationships, supply chain relationships between the firms on the chain, employee to employee and employee to management relationships within an organization. Human relationships have such a huge impact. Production and operations run smoothly because of the lubrication of relationships.

Materials Requirement Planning (MRP)

The above discussion also points towards another major culprit in the inventories – for that matter in the entire

POM – which is 'uncertainty'. JIT minimizes uncertainty by having committed deliveries just in time from its suppliers and other input. Eliminate uncertainty and a big job is done. We take the help of Statistics because we want to find 'order within the apparent disorder and uncertainty'. That is the way we want to get a hold on uncertainty and deal with it.

However, sometimes, we may be overdoing 'statistics'. When the demand for an item can be computed based on the requirement of the higher (more aggregated) item, why should one refer to statistics? Such items are called 'dependent demand' items. A considerable percentage of items in manufacturing are in fact such 'dependent demand' items. From the quantity of desks to be made available by a certain date, we can compute the number of desk-tops that should be made, which in turn tells us the number/quantity of plywood sheets to be had and by which date. This simple arithmetical computation for the requirements of various intermediate and raw materials is termed 'Materials Requirement Planning (MRP)'. The advantage with MRP is that it is a direct computation of the amounts required. Why create uncertainty when it does not exist?

Statistics would have used our fear levels or what is termed as 'service levels'. If ten items were to get into a pharmaceutical formulation, and if we would have used 95 per cent 'service level' (seems reasonably high, isn't it?), the mathematical probability of all these ten ingredients to be available at the same time is: $0.95 \times 0.95 \times 0.95 \times 0.95 \times 0.95 \times 0.95 \times 0.95 \times 0.95 \times 0.95 \times 0.95 = 0.60$. This is quite low. Surprised? We should know how to interpret statistics and when to use it.

Principle 14:
Use Statistics Wisely.
Know when to use
and
How to interpret.

MRP concept is now used at the organizational level and various resources – not just material – and end results are tracked, computed and planned. This is called Enterprise Resource Planning (ERP). Information Technology is used in order to get a time to time picture of the state of affairs.

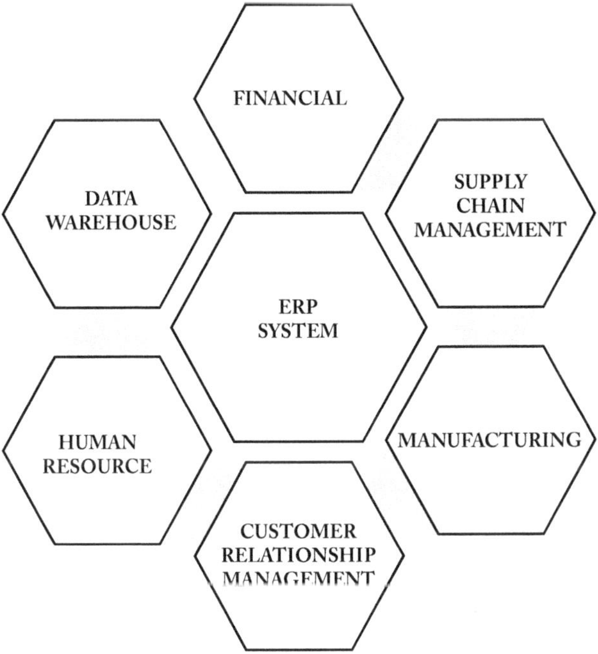

FIG. 6: ERP

Internet of Things and Industry 4.0

The basic message of ERP is: 'Be Connected on a Real Time Basis'. That is the message for the Operations Management system and a 'mantra' for the entire enterprise. In this connectivity, the Internet is going to play a huge role in the very near future. Already, we are entering into the Internet of Things (IoT), a revolutionary technology connecting all 'things' (materials, machines, men and management). The connection will be between people-people, people-things and things-things. Anything that can be connected, will be connected!

The advantages of connecting things are unimaginably high. For the present, we can imagine that our operations system would know when it was running low on supplies and will automatically re-order more. The system would know where the item/material is needed when and would automatically send it. In a more developed state, the Operations Management system will be like – or a lot better than – the 'auto pilot' of today's planes. The job of the management persons will be to set the direction for the enterprise and the operations system and intervene only when 'exceptions' are encountered; the other important job for the management will be to understand the 'human' dimension/feelings/emotions and deal with those, i.e. do what 'things' cannot do and only humans can. Things will connect; people will relate.

The future will see amazing increase in data volumes, computational/analytical power, connectivity, and in transferring digital instructions to the physical world, such as advanced robotics and 3-D printing. Today we are labeling these developments under one phrase: Industry 4.0, a fancy word for the fourth industrial revolution.

The revolutionary principle is about the power of connectivity.

Principle 15
Be connected.
Exchange information between all members/things of the enterprise family.

Unimaginable amounts of improvements will be seen in not only managing materials inventories but in overall speed, agility and quality of service deliveries.

Of course, when gateways of information are open, there is always a threat of unwanted intruders peeping in and listening. Privacy and security are the major concerns in IoT, especially information sharing. Security should be an intrinsic part while designing/developing devices and applications when things and people are interconnected.

Chapter 10

Quality

What is Quality? Who defines it? User or producer or both? Some define quality as: Perform as promised. 'Promise' again, is perceived through the eyes of the customer. Customer perception is the ultimate.

First you find out what the customer wants. What is a 'good quality' product/service or a range of such products/services for him/her?

Then you choose/decide to offer him/her a product/service accordingly. So, you decide on the parameters that are to be provided. This is your 'quality strategy'.

Does your product/service perform whatever you are up to? Does the performance consistently match the promise (to yourself and/or to the customer)? If it does, you have produced a 'good quality' product/service. The basic aspect of quality is about prevention of non-conformance to the desired/set standard/s.

Sometimes, you may like to exceed the expectations or desires of the customer. Thus, you may like to 'delight' the customer. 'Sone pe suhaagaa' as a Hindi adage goes. Or, 'Dudhaat saakhar padli' as per a Marathi adage, for exceeding expectations.

Consider the following example of *Puran Poli*.

Quality in Making *Puran Poli*

Say you are a good cook. You want to invite your friends and satisfy their desire for a home-made sweet. You know or find out that they love a traditional sweet like *Puran Poli* (also called Obbattu in Kannada/Telugu), one which can be carried home and stored for a few days. So, you decide on your 'product strategy': *Puran Poli* as a sweet dish and gift, something they can carry back home.

Step1: Explore Customer Needs and Decide on Quality

What do the customers (your friends) expect in a *Puran Poli*? You list them:

- The stuffing should be of *gram dhal* (*chana daal*) and jaggery.
- *Poli* should be thin. But, it should not be very thin, like those available in the neighboring stores. The sweet *puran* should be in sufficient quantity in each *Poli*.
- The covering of the *Poli* should not break and open out the stuffed *Puran*. So, it should be made of '*Maida*' (fine wheat flour with very little roughage).
- *Poli* should be crisp. So, a small proportion of fine *Rava* (broken wheat) has to be added to the kneaded flour.

Based on the above, the ingredients have been decided for 'operation *puran poli*'. You know that the *daal* should be of a particular variety and quality generally available in the local supermarket. Jaggery should be the type that is exported, neither the 'yellow cubes' nor the round hard elliptical balls. Since Poli has to be crisp, a small proportion of fine *Rava* (broken wheat) needs to be added to the kneaded flour. You also need a small quantity of refined sunflower oil for shallow frying and two tea-spoonfuls of cardamom powder for flavoring. Thus, you standardize the ingredients.

Step 2: Standardize Ingredients

Jaggery Chana Daal Maida Thin Rava
Oil Cardamom

The process has to be standardized. This involves taking *maida* in a predetermined quantity and kneading it with pre-decided (small) amount of water and cooking oil (refined sunflower oil).

It also involves cooking the *gram dhal* (*chana daal*) of pre-decided quantity in a pressure cooker until the *daal* is very soft. It is to be mashed in mixer-grinder until it is smooth. The jaggery (pre-decided quantity) is to be melted separately in another vessel. The moment it melts, the mashed *chana daal* is to be added and blended along with the pre-decided quantity of cardamom powder. The result of this process is the '*puran*'. Let it cool to room temperature. Make several balls of pre-decided size.

Step 3: Standardize the Process (all the steps)

Now make correct size of kneaded flour. Roll it to a particular size. Stuff the *puran* ball and complete the covering. On a butter paper, roll it to a particular thickness (thin-ness).

Keep the skillet pre-heated on low flame. Transfer the rolled *poli*. Bake for two minutes on one side. Flip and bake for one-and-half minute on the other side. Brush a thin layer of cooking oil and bake for half a minute more on each side. Dark brown big spots should have appeared on a golden *poli*.

Step 4: Involve the People (your associates)

You cannot do all the work that is involved. You involve some of your neighbor friends and/or your spouse. Each one should know their role. The more 'drilled' and 'involved' they are, the more perfect is the quality. Their work needs standardization. Of course, they can suggest many small improvements as they practice more. Japanese, who produce excellent quality goods, have a term for such small improvements; it is called "Kaizen".

Step 5: Suggestions and 'Kaizen'

Serve the *poli* warm to your guests (friends).

Step 6: Delight the customers

Delight them by giving them a choice of warm milk or molten *ghee* (clarified butter) on their *puran poli.*

Would you be able to deliver the same quality next time, and over and over again? That depends on standardizing the ingredients; also on you having standardized the process (all detailed steps), thoroughly trained your associates, motivating them to be watchful of any errors or variations, improving the process through their suggestions as they gain repeat experience. The ultimate aim is to satisfy the customers and keep improving it. A lot depends upon your and your associates' intense desire to do so. Call it 'culture', call it 'values' or 'mission'.

Service Quality Model

Some interesting queries from the above *Puran Poli* making are as follows.

Was there a gap between what the customers (your *invitees*) *expected* from you and what *they experienced*? This gap; the ultimate gap, needs to be addressed.

Was there a gap to start with, in what *you thought* invitees expected (your plan for quality) and what the *invitees actually expected?* This was a gap in your quality planning.

Narrative 1:

> Invitees telling each other, 'Oh, oh! Expected her to make *puran poli* out of *Tuvar Daal*; she has made it out of *Chana Daal* like the Maharashtrians make.'

Gap 1

Was there a gap between your *plan for quality* and your *translation* of it *into* the *specifications*? This is the translation gap.

Narrative 2:

> You (hostess) thinking: 'Did not tell my friend how soft the *daal* for the *puran* should have cooked. I will specify the next time I make the *poli*.'

Gap 2

Was there a gap between the *specifications* and the *delivery* of the service/*poli*? This is the delivery gap.

Narrative 3:

> You (hostess) thinking: 'Had told my husband to bake the *poli* on one side for two minutes; he over-baked a little due to oversight.'

Gap 3

Was there a gap between what the invitees were *told* and what was *delivered* to them? This is the communication gap.

Narrative 4:

> Invitees telling each other, 'She had told us it would be a home-made sweet. Indeed, it is so.'

Gap 4

The first gap (we called it the 'ultimate' one; do not confuse with Gap 1) is the result of all the other gaps which we should try to close. This is the gap between the *customers' expectations* and *their experience*. This is also called Gap 5.

Narrative 5:

> Invitees telling each other, 'Delightfully different experience! Although the *puran poli* was made of *Chana Daal*.'

Gap 5

This seemingly simple description of improving quality is actually a powerful concept. It is called the *Service Quality Model*.

Total Quality Management

Did you notice? You have almost performed a Total Quality Management (TQM) exercise in making *Puran Poli*. Organizations, whether they are small (like our house) or very huge, run on the same basic principles.

What did you notice as the basic principles?

- ♠ A **culture** of *providing/serving the very best*.
  - **Customer focus** to know what s/he wants.
    - ◆ Based on it decide and **specify** the result to be achieved in all dimensions of quality, and
    - ◆ Specify all the steps that lead to that result
  - Fault-less execution of all the steps (**minimize variations**)
    - ◆ Standardize – processes, actions taken, materials
    - ◆ Train all people in the process
    - ◆ Involve all people in the process
- ♠ **Keep improving**
  - the inculcation of the organizational values in the total enterprise

- the customer focus
- the involvement of the people
- the product and the service
- the process
  - the method
  - the technology
  - the machines
  - the skills

Mark the important words or

The Basic principles of Quality:

♠Instill or Create a Culture of Customer Focus in the Organization

♠Specify – Expected results and All the necessary Actions

♠Minimize variations

♠Keep on Improving

Principle 16: Culture of Customer Focus.
Quality arises from the culture of the organization.

Quality arises from the culture of the organization. Therefore, much of TQM exercise is to align the culture of the organization to the needs of the customers; and then, aligning everybody – in or associated with the organization – to the organization's culture.

Such focus on customer tells the organization what service/products it should deliver and what standards it should set for the same.

Minimizing variations from the set standards is the goal in quality. The interacting things are: Men, Materials and Machines. These 3 M's generate quality.

Machines Men Materials

FIG. 7: 3 M's that Generate Quality

Total Quality Management (TQM) believes in fortifying all the above three generators of quality. It is 'total' in that sense.

Men: Much of the 'Quality' is in the mind. Once a quality is thought of (or devised) or the Destination for quality is decided, it depends much upon Determination and Discipline (call it culture, if you will) of those, who have to deliver quality.

Therefore, reduce human variations (thus improve quality) by:

- Motivating them and involving them to keep reducing their own errors/variations. Quality Circles is one such effort.

  Quality Circles
  Volunteers (numbering anywhere from three to fifteen) from the workers form a group and meet regularly weekly or bi-weekly for about an hour or more in order to identify, analyze and search for solutions in work-related problems and the ways of

implementing the solutions. Japanese organizations pioneered this simple and effective concept of employee participation and involvement.

- Aligning interacting humans to the organization's culture; these people could be your employees and your vendors in the supply chain.
- Training them so that:
  Each one knows his/her precise role/job.
  Each one knows how that job is to be done without error.
  Each one is mentally aligned; and so:
  - Each one knows why it is being done the way it is to be done.
  - Each one knows about the overall goal of the whole activity i.e. the larger organizational goal or the larger scheme of things.
- Making processes fool-proof wherever it is possible to do so.

Since we gave an example of preparing a food item earlier, let us continue with another similar example of infusing 'Quality' in a 'service' operation.

Example of a Restaurant

In the restaurant of a 5-Star hotel, the Chef, the Sous Chef, the Junior Sous Chef, the person who takes the order, the bearer who serves the dish to the customer and waits on the table – all of these personnel's must know their precise task allocation.

Each one must also know how it should be done, in an error-free manner.

They must know what they should not do i.e. what constitutes an error and of what scale.

They must also be aware of the larger scheme of things – the principles of customer service that the restaurant/hotel holds dear.

From welcoming the guests to the restaurant, getting them to be comfortably seated at the table, taking their order, conveying it to the kitchen, executing the same i.e. preparing the dish, plating (garnishing), presenting the dish to the guest, serving and waiting on the table, clearing the table when the guest finishes eating, bill presentation, to seeing the guest off – are a number of tasks that should have been practiced like a drill. It should be so perfected that no one should make any error, at any time.

Fool proofing should be used wherever possible. For instance, in Barbeque Nation (a chain of restaurants), vegetarian clients are identified by serving them in green rimmed dinner plates. So, the error of serving a non-vegetarian food item to a vegetarian guest never occurs. In India, that would be a major error and would spoil the entire dinner party for the guests.

FIG. 8: 'Serving' Process: from order taking to presenting the dish to the guest

And despite abundant precaution and practice, if an error does occur, the person/s concerned should know how to rectify it. They should know how to make the best of the bad situation.

Machine:

Product or service is produced/provided by the use of an equipment or a set of equipments.

Reduce variations by means of:

- Automation/Robotics/Computerization i.e. using improved technology.
  Computers do their job from a distance; robots do not get fatigued and can work in harsh environments unlike humans. They are capable of extremely precise and repetitive work.
- Eliminate/minimize machine errors by Total Productive Maintenance (TPM).

More on Total Productive Maintenance (TPM) in the next chapter.

The idea behind TQM is that the vendors supply the right quality of materials, the employees carry out their assigned duties flawlessly, and the machines operate without errors. Every link in the chain of activities does its assigned function without error. There is the 'quality script' which is orchestrated. The final effect is that the customers, the audience, the patrons are satisfied and happy.

So, what is the big message in Total Quality Management? At the risk of repetition, the message is that Quality cannot be just 'controlled' from outside. It is generated from within. That is why the organization culture and the preparation of all people are so important.

FIG. 9: Principle of Quality: Involve people and Get them to work in a team

For a very long time in the twentieth century, we were stuck in the concept of 'controlling' quality with the (mis)use of statistics – a science of numbers the world had recently discovered then. Statistics is good; but quality demands more than the use of statistics. It needs people's involvement, their focus on the customer, their determination and discipline.

Getting off the magical spell of 3

Old concept of quality was to control the process and see that the errors are within the statistical three sigma limits. For several decades, the figure three (in three sigma) had an enduring hold on the minds of people. Frankly, it was thought to be a short-cut to 'quality'.

A generation or two ago, people were enamored of the rapid production capability of machines. Short-cut production had to have a short-cut to 'quality'.

If a machine that was cranking out an item, made a spread of +/-1.35 'off-quality' items i.e. a total of about 3 (2.7 to be more exact) 'defectives' per thousand produced, it was acceptable to the operations managers then. That was within the control limits of 3-sigma. They said, it was in the 'normal' behavior of any machine. Same was true of human beings; workers were anyway thought of as extensions of machines.

Today the requirements of quality are high. In most operations today, we cannot tolerate '3 (or 2.7 to be more exact) defectives in 1000' kind of quality. The number of defectives of 2700 per million (called ppm) is considered 'terrible' quality today. That is a horrendously huge number of defectives rate. Quality control in terms of 'Percent defectives' is history. Modern business is too complex and old ideas about 'acceptable quality level' can no longer be tolerated.

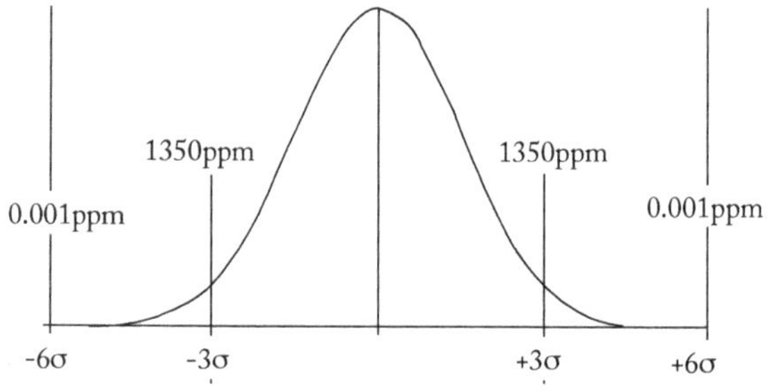

FIG. 10: Three-Sigma (3σ) and Six-Sigma (6σ) Limits under the Normal Distribution and the corresponding Defectives

People are talking of Six Sigma limits today; this means 0.002 ppm defects or 'Two defects per billion interactions' type of quality. Even if we consider that, in practice, the process mean can drift 1.5 sigma in either direction over a period of time (as Motorola, a leader in Six Sigma movement presumed), this translates to a maximum defectives rate of 3.4 ppm. (Compare this to the old 3-sigma control limits:

considering the drift, the defectives rate would have been 66.8 per 1,000 i.e. 66,800 ppm which is extremely huge.)

Modern business requires near-perfect quality levels. TQM does not speak of Six Sigma limits. But, it talks of attaining near-perfection i.e. minimizing error through organizational culture and the preparation of people.

> **Principle 17:**
> **Strive to Attain Perfection.**
> **Quality is about Near Perfection.**
> **Specify results and actions**
> **and**
> **Minimize variations.**

Six Sigma

This is a more recent quality movement that believes in specifying the exacting Six Sigma requirements as against the TQM movement which is not so explicit.

The fit between organization's culture and customer requirements, the customer focus, process specification, and skills training, information and knowledge for the people (employees and business associates) are the same as in TQM. Only difference is: every process has to be brought to Six Sigma level capabilities.

Six Sigma capabilities would mean a lot of discipline, training, drill, involvement and commitment on the part of all, so that errors are almost non-existent. Machines and supporting equipment also need to be inherently good and maintained well so as to produce Six Sigma quality. Input materials also need to be of exactingly consistent quality.

Six Sigma is excellent about 'prevention of non-conformance'. However, the organization should not get trapped in statistics or numbers once again. As TQM says, quality is also about delighting the customer through continuous improvement and innovation.

Chapter 11

Managing Maintenance

If the machines do not operate faultlessly, there will be problems in the quality of the output. Also, the 'flow' of production operations will be disturbed. The quality and quantity of output will be affected if breakdowns; major or minor, occur. Therefore, error-free operations of the machines are desirable.

When a breakdown occurs in the manufacturing industry, it shall be fixed by replacing the damaged parts or the equipment itself. This is called 'breakdown maintenance'. That consumes time – the essential resource – and involves expenditure of effort. A breakdown also means a wastage of the material in process. More importantly, breakdowns arrive unexpectedly; they do not come with a schedule. There is negative surprise element in a breakdown; because the breakdown disturbs the rhythm of operations. It is not one operation, but a number of them – that were to accompany it and many to follow – would be affected. Therefore, breakdowns should be rare; and the incidences of breakdown maintenance (BM) should be minimal.

Services can be very 'fragile'. If something breaks down with a service operation or if an error occurs, to mend it, i.e. to win back the trust of the customers is a rather tough task. Imagine the following happening to a reputed restaurant; a lady customer is frazzled and is screaming when she notices a cockroach in the plate. Customers on other tables too are getting up shocked. Would a 'breakdown maintenance' action such as replacing the dish, even for free, help heal the damage?

It would be a wise business policy to ensure that breakdown maintenance is a rare occurrence in service operations.

In certain process and engineering industries, breakdown maintenance is no maintenance at all. What is the point in blowing up a pipe in either a nuclear power plant or in a poisonous insecticide factory and then attend to breakdown maintenance however efficiently?

Preventive Maintenance

Towards this, the machines need to be maintained in order to prevent a breakdown. Preventive maintenance (PM) action – monitoring the condition of critical equipment by continuously checking certain parameters like temperature rise or pressure build-up, general actions like inspecting, lubricating, and the preventive replacement of parts – is indispensable towards preventing the deterioration or a sudden breakdown of the machines. Preventive action is equally or more important in service operations as that in the manufacturing industries.

Know Where the Problem Is:

Things fail because of three basic reasons:

1. They get worn out and fail and die, like aging wears out humans.
2. They are tripped and so they fail, like accidents will incapacitate humans.
3. They have a design defect and fail in early working, like human young ones with weaknesses at birth may be more prone to disease right from the early years. As the years roll by, the breakdowns may reduce as the system settles.

There is no point in focusing on an equipment when the problem is the wildly fluctuating power voltages; the problem here is external to the equipment. That has to be attended.

If there are faults in the way a machine has been assembled or designed, preventive replacement would not be as effective as correcting the design itself.

If a graph is drawn of the failure probability of an equipment to its age, it will show a sharp dip in the beginning, a fairly constant rate in the middle, and a sharp rise in the later ages. The graph looks like the pencil sketch of a bath tub; hence it is called a 'bath tub curve'.

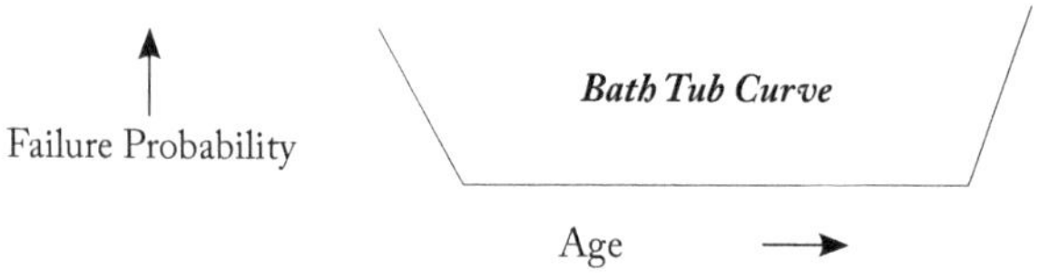

FIG. 11: Bath Tub Curve

Whatever may be the reason, a breakdown has to be attended to immediately. However, if preventive action is to be taken, it has to target the appropriate cause – internal or external. Bath tub curve draws our attention to the fact that the cause of failure could be wear-out or an inherent design defect or something outside the equipment system.

Reliability considerations

The idea behind 'preventive maintenance' is to enhance the reliability of the operations equipment / operations system.

An equipment or an operation is said to be 'reliable' if, as a system, it keeps doing the intended job for a given time span under specified environment or use conditions.

Do note that an equipment may fail (stop, slow down or hinder quality) when a single component fails. As is commonly known: a chain is only as strong as its weakest link. One may also notice that a team can fail if it has a weak member.

A family's reputation is, in many cases, only as good as that of its least reputed member. There is a simple mathematical expression for this phenomenon.

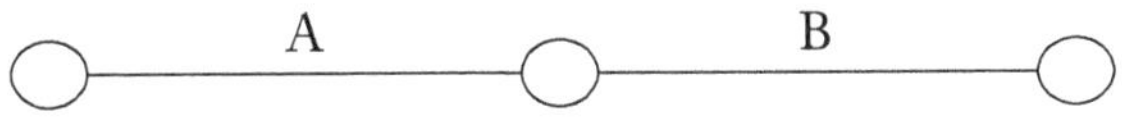

Reliability of A & B joined in series = (Reliability of A) × (Reliability of B)

Since any reliability cannot exceed 1.0, the reliability of A & B is lower than that of either A or B. The weak link can drag the reliability down. This is an important consideration in maintenance.

But, if a link/component is added as a stand-by, or something or someone who will take over if and when the first link fails, then the result is enhanced reliability.

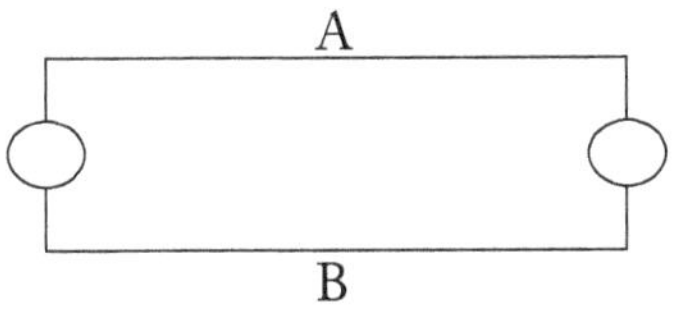

Reliability of A & B joined in parallel =

1 – (1- Reliability of A) × (1 – Reliability of B) =

$1-(1-R_A-R_B+R_A.R_B)=R_A+R_B-R_A.R_B$

When two components are joined in parallel, the combined reliability is higher than that of each of the individual components.

There is a larger message or principle involved in this:

> **Principle 18**
> **Do not just link up.**
> **Be supportive.**
> **Together, you will then be more invincible.**

Putting parts and people in 'parallel' makes all the difference. Imagine you are learning how to drive a car. Your spouse is sitting next to you. If the spouse only frightens you as you take turns at every lane, it will make you even less confident of driving as compared to your usual self. In your anxiety, you are more prone to accident or breakdown. Instead, if your supportive spouse says, 'You are doing good! Driving really good. Don't worry. I will take over whenever you want me to', it will strengthen you.

Maintainability Improvement

It would be desirable that the maintenance actions, breakdown maintenance and preventive maintenance, take as little time as possible. If possible, they should not cut into the operation time. The loss in operation time, because of maintenance, should be as little as possible. Thus, there should be a focus on 'Maintainability Improvement (MI)' whereby maintenance actions are easier to perform. Better MI means easier BM and PM.

Maintenance Prevention

In fact, maintenance considerations should be proactive in nature. Emphasis should be on Maintenance Prevention (MP) i.e. having a maintenance-free design. Problems should not occur, in the first place. Actually, this has much application in the 'service' industry where infallibility and being proactive are vital.

A service operations example:

An airline should not misplace or lose luggage. When it does, it has to attend to that 'breakdown' immediately and in all earnestness. A passenger's 'missed' bag has to be retrieved and returned to him urgently and with sincere apologies and courtesy. This is similar to 'breakdown maintenance'.

There should be efficient processes to trace the lost bags and to interact courteously with the affected customer; that would 'improve maintainability'.

However, systems should be in place to prevent such an error by the ground staff and handling personnel through regular training programs – in brushing up on procedures and in honing up attitude – and by periodically rotating 'rusty' personnel to other jobs. This is akin to 'preventive maintenance'.

Even better would be to design systems that are fool-proof – such that the human element is minimized, if not eliminated, and there is no need to train or retrain the staff. This would be 'maintenance prevention'.

We see that in services, people/staff are as much or more important than physical equipment. Breakdowns occur because of a failure to follow the carefully laid out procedures or systems. Sometimes parts of the system would have become worn out (or obsolete) over time and need a fresh replacement. Sometimes, there may be an overload on the service operations and the operations may trip or fail because of it. At other times, the design of the system itself may be flawed right from the beginning. Principles of 'maintenance' in service operations are no different than those in the manufacturing operations.

Principle 19
It is said that 'A Stitch in Time Saves Nine': Avoid breakdowns. Hence, take preventive action.

But, why have a stitch in the first place? Eliminate the need for any maintenance action – preventive or other.

A pair of jeans made of denim is a good example of the above principle. Perhaps, the genesis of jeans was in the need in the rough and tough of the wild west, for a garment that did not need any maintenance – breakdown or preventive.

Maintenance and Quality and Productivity

Maintenance and quality are so inter-related and similar. A companywide involvement (autonomous maintenance) by operators and small group activities concerning maintenance by departments such as engineering, logistics and marketing would go a long way. There would be a lot more feeling of ownership of maintaining operations equipment and operations systems.

Total Productive Maintenance (TPM)

All the above actions – preventive maintenance, maintainability improvement, maintenance prevention and companywide involvement – together constitute what is known as Total Productive Maintenance (TPM).

With TPM implementation, the operations will be expected to have:

- no breakdowns
- no short stoppages or slow-downs
- no defectives and
- no safety breaches and mishaps – big or small.

The operations would be helped to become fully productive. More on productivity in the next chapter.

Chapter 12

Productivity Concepts

Productivity, in its basic definition, is the ratio of the 'quantity of output per unit of input'.

We are generally anxious to know what we ***get*** for what we ***put*** in.

What we *put* in could be various things: Rupees of investment, hours of effort, kWh of energy, Kilogram of material, bushels of cow-feed, liter of petrol in a car and so on.

What we *get* could consist of any of the outputs like: Rupees of revenue, number of foot-falls in a shop, number of visitors to a website, Kilogram of product, liters of milk, mileage of a car and so on.

Rupees of Revenue *per* Rupee of Investment, Kilogram of product *per* kWh of energy, Viewership numbers on digital media *per* Rupee of investment, Mileage *per* liter of petrol and so on are ratios representing 'productivity' in those particular situations.

Better, Quicker, Smarter and a Winner

In a Twenty-20 Cricket match we may judge a batsman by various ways, like:

Number of runs scored to the number of times batted:
*(How **good** is he at scoring runs?)*

Number of runs per number of balls faced
*(How **quick** is he in scoring runs?)*

Number of sixes and fours hit to the number of times batted
*(How **smart** is he while batting? How frightening could he be to the opposite team?)*

Number of times judged as a man of the match to the number of matches batted
*(Is he a **match-winner**?)*

Each one of the above ratios tells us a different story about how 'productive' that batter (batsman/batswoman) has been.

Even all the above four ratios do not narrate the entire tale of the usefulness of the batsman. A batsman may perform great service to his team by standing at the crease and giving support to the batsmen hitting sixes from the other end. Productivity is needed in this world in various ways.

Each one of the ratios as given above is a Partial Productivity measure. Productivity is generally measured in several partial measures. Of course, one could combine a few and get a Multi-Factor Productivity measure. Like when we see an elephant in its multiple aspects, we see the 'real' (at least nearer its 'reality') elephant. Partial measures might have given us only its tail (small mammal?) or its long trunk (a python?) or its legs (rubbery columns?).

Productivity as Team-work

Twenty-20 cricket matches also tell us that while individual productivity is good to have, the total productivity is a team effort. You cannot win a match unless you put in a team effort.

Likewise, in manufacturing plants and in service sector operations, human workforce is viewed, not just as individuals manning appointed work-stations but as a team for the larger goal to be achieved. That goal could be a particular product to be made of acceptable quality;

or even a hospital where patients have to be treated and healed. Productivity is, ultimately, the sum of the various parts to make a whole.

Productivity Improvement is about Looking at the Trees and also the Forest

The pursuit of productivity is about getting better and better outcomes. Some outcomes are not entirely quantifiable. Like say: 'enhance the value to the customer' or 'enhance competitiveness of the organization' or 'steer the organization in the right direction'. Or for instance, 'increased confidence of the small farmers' or 'enhanced empowerment of women'. But these outcomes are highly impacting and therefore very important. Therefore, when we think of productivity, we must not only think of 'efficiency' but also of holistic 'effectiveness' and 'impact'. Productivity should look at the trees as well as at the forest.

Productivity as Socio-economic Impact

While 'productivity' is a very important consideration in manufacturing and service enterprises in the private sector, it is as much or a shade more important when dealing with social and public projects and programs, which have a far-reaching impact on a large swathe of population.

Lack of adequate productivity in the construction of a power project, affects the economy of a province or a country for a long time – for decades, as we are familiar with India's power projects that were delayed despite spending the stipulated funds. In fact, most projects faced huge cost over-runs in addition to or as a consequence of time over-runs. As per one calculation (done in 1988), if India's power projects had completed on time, the GDP of the country would have been three-fold then. Imagine the roll-over effect three decades later (now)?

FIG. 12: Far-reaching Impacts of a Hydel Power Plant on other activities like Factories, Schools, Hospitals, and Railways

Imagine another government project like Polio eradication; a health sector project. The longer it takes to complete, the worse it gets. The social cost of lame children and adults due to the communicable disease has been horrendously huge. It is only just a few years ago, that our country was declared polio-free.

In such a program, productivity is required on several fronts: Productivity in *communicating to the rural people* the importance of immunization against poliomyelitis (this was a Himalayan task); productivity in *allaying their fears* about polio vaccine; productivity in making/*obtaining* the vaccine; productivity in *transporting* the vaccine to different nooks and corners of the country; productivity in maintaining the *cold chain* (i.e. maintaining the quality of the vaccine over a long time); productivity of village level healthcare workers to *identify* the infants and babies; productivity in *maintaining the required schedule of vaccination* over the first few years in the life of the babies; productivity in *retaining rural and slum area health staff* like doctors, nurses, auxiliary nurses, midwives; productivity in *not missing any target* (i.e. baby) in any year, amongst many other measures.

In such cases, productivity is less about the ratio of output to input and more about the output itself. The government may spend less or more funds; however, the ultimate objective is to get the desired results at the appointed time.

How to enhance productivity?

Productivity depends on the methods, processes, systems, equipment, techniques and technologies of operations. Improvement in any of these factors may improve productivity – through minimizing the resources used or through the output being enhanced, or both.

In order to know whether the quantity of output is OK, better, best or worse, we must know what is OK or normally expected quantity of output in a specified time duration.

Time Study

For instance, as a small-time restaurateur, I should know in how much time a *Masala Dosa can* be prepared and served. If I know that it usually takes ten minutes, this gives me an idea of what I should promise the customer, and how much I could improve on the time aspect, if necessary.

Same holds true for factories. The manager of a garment factory should know how much time it 'normally' takes to stitch a collar for a shirt. The manager can then think of ways to improve (reduce) the time. Therefore, we see that we need to assess the normal time to make and deliver a *Dosa* or to stitch a shirt-collar. This assessment is called as 'Time Study'.

We can use a stop-watch to check on the time. We may time the smaller elements of work in making the *Dosa* and add them up – like wiping the *tawa* (pan), spreading the batter, putting the *Masala* on the Dosa, flipping the *Dosa* into the attractive shape onto the dish, *arranging* chutney in the dish, and the bearer carrying the dish to the table of the guest. We may mentally assess at what efficiency are all these tasks being performed – called 'performance rating' and give an appropriate correction to arrive at the total time estimate. The procedure and the logic behind it are simple.

Many of the industrial jobs and their micro-elements have already been standardized. There is no need to measure them again. These are called 'synthetic' time standards.

For instance, you are having your breakfast and want to sprinkle salt and pepper on your omlette; how much time will it take? The salt and pepper shakers are placed atop the dining table. We can breakdown the component elements of tasks; their respective normal times are also 'synthetically' available in the Methods Time Measurement (MTM-1) system. These are given below.

Table 1: An Example Using Synthetic (MTM) Times*

Motion Elements	*Time in Time Measurement Units (TMU)# for Each Shaker*	
Reach 12 inches	12.9	
Grasp shaker	8.7	
Transport 12 inches	13.4	
Eye focus & travel	22.5	
Position above plate	19.7	
Shake 2 inch 12 times (up & down)	4.6 × 12 × 2	**This is just an example. Not an exact version.*
Transport 12 inches	13.4	*# In MTM system, 1 TMU = 0.00001 hour.*
Eye focus & travel	22.5	
Position	19.7	
Release	2.0	
	245.2 TMU	

TOTAL (for 2 shakers): 245.2 TMU × 2 = 0.004904 hour = 17.65 seconds. This is 'Normal Time'.

Considering that one may not be extremely active early morning, one may be given an allowance of, say, 20 per cent. In which case, the Standard Time would be 17.65/(1 – 0.20) = 22.06= 22 seconds (approximately).

Time standards form the basis of any improvement in productivity.

Methods Study

We may check the method or the flow of the process in a little more detail and modify these to improve on time. These improvements are called Method Study and Process Flow Study. In offices, the time to process a paper may depend significantly on the organization of the office; hence the term Organization and Methods (O&M) study.

Industrial Engineers

A few decades ago, there was much less automation. The repetitive jobs performed by the workers had to be measured for arriving at the 'standard time' for each of the jobs. That was the way to control the output from the workers; trade unions and managements had to agree on the time standards. There were specialist engineers – called 'Industrial Engineers' – who would help set these time standards and in standardizing the methods and processes.

Equipment Maintenance and Automation

Maintain the equipment and the equipment will produce the desired quality of output at the pre-set rate of production. When breakdowns and the downtimes are minimized, the productivity is obviously maximized. As noted in the earlier chapter, Total Productive Maintenance (TPM) aims to minimize the disruptions and hence, maximizes productivity.

Automation minimizes the human element and therefore, minimizes human fatigue and fallibility. Automation makes for quick corrective action. Also, repeatability could vastly improve. Accuracy, precision and quality of output could improve with automation.

Humans need not do hazardous jobs and therefore, there is increased safety. Speed of output could be considerably more. So, there could be a multifarious enhancement in productivity.

Role of Men

Did we forget 'men'? Certainly not. Productivity is very much about humans that are involved – training, skilling and motivating them. Humans are there to work on the machines, supervise and maintain them.

And the morale of men/women needs to be maintained. Hence, organizations believe in having equitable or fair systems of wages and salaries. For this reason, they have Job Evaluation studies done so that wage scales are decided based on job difficulties and responsibilities.

People do like to make extra money. Monetary inducement (External Motivation) can make people interested in work; and work more and quicker. Therefore, some organizations design Financial Incentive plans and Overtime (OT) payment plans. For positions where the output is not tangible, they devise inducements like Employee Stock Option Plans (ESOP) and other financial benefits. However, organizations understand that the effect of financial inducement on improved productivity has limits.

At times, financial incentives could give rise to a mismatch: Employees may produce enhanced output when the demands are actually low; the enterprise may end up having a large inventory of work-in-process items.

Therefore, the organizations try to improve the drive of the employees by making the job more interesting by means of Job Enlargement (increasing responsibilities) and Job Enrichment (including higher level responsibilities in the job). Promotions in the job are a method of appreciating good work.

But, many of the above actions – particularly those involving financial aspects – are fraught with the risk of setting up undesirable competition between the employees. This can be counter-productive.

Misdirected efforts could prove disastrous

One has to be careful that the whole exercise of productivity is not for 'appearances sake'. It is easy to take shelter under numbers and ratios. Top management has to ensure that there is 'right intent' behind the efforts; and it has to ensure its proper implementation.

During the 'Emergency period' during 1975-77, the Government of India had a program of voluntary Male Sterilization with a long-term intention of controlling the burgeoning population. However, the message regarding 'voluntary' vasectomies did not get spread effectively. Since the productivity of the Health staff was measured in terms of number of vasectomies performed, they performed vasectomies on very old persons and in many cases repeatedly, while the young male villagers hid in the farms to avoid getting vasectomy done on them.

Business Process Reengineering (BPR)

An important lesson in productivity is that one should think *beyond* the problem. If we try to find solutions at the level of the problem, we tend to get palliative solutions; sometimes no solution at all or worse – a misdirected response. A bird's eye view may help.

A fundamental rethink about why our organization does the things the way it does is called Business Process Reengineering. It is a deep introspection; and then overhauling and redesigning the existing processes from scratch. As mentioned earlier, improved methods, systems and technologies may help improve productivity. But, a periodic deep introspection would keep the enterprise in line with the right objectives. Households, businesses, governments – all of these need such an exercise.

Quality and Productivity

You might have noticed that the fundamental lessons of quality and those of productivity are very similar. Improved quality and improved productivity arise as much out of technological advances, as out of the total commitment of the people involved in that business, program or project.

While the management provides the necessary customer focus and provides the leadership to create the organizational environment, it is the people at other levels who work in line with the objectives and in accordance with the 'script' and deliver the service and/or the product.

Principle 20:
Transform Ordinary into Extraordinary

Employees should have training, information, knowledge and skills. That is the basic requirement. But something more is required. Productivity and quality – in business and in government or in any other activities – are about pursuing excellence. It is about making ordinary persons connected to the task/business/program into extra-ordinary people. Nothing short of Popeye who has eaten spinach.

Organizations need to encourage, rather incubate, excellence. An excellent plumber is as admirable as a competent philosopher. A society that promotes excellence will have its theories that hold water just as would its pipes.

Chapter 13

Future

Will Production and Operations Management change substantially in the future? The basic principles will hardly change. Grandma's recipes and her core principles of tasty cooking remain substantially unchanged.

The available technology and the level of automation is very likely to change. Like, she too, uses piped/cooking gas and electric oven. It makes her life easier. She too, can check on the internet once in a way to see what others are cooking. She too, can dish out a pizza or pasta once in a way.

New Implements

In industry – manufacturing or other, with the advances in computer and communications technology, the humans are being tremendously helped in operations. In commercial aircraft, auto-pilots are used. The human pilots are there; but they are substantially relieved of continuous navigation and other tasks; the tiresome drudgery is removed. Technological advances will take away the grind, but the human oversight, giving a sense of general direction and ultimate control will always be there. With increased input of technology, the need for oversight might become a little more acute.

Let us see what else may change with increasing technology. By the next decade, self-driven automobiles will become a common sight. With the advent of auto-driven cars of the future, the human-driven city-taxis and human-driven ridesharing app-based cabs will substantially reduce. People will give a command and the auto-driven car will drive them safely to their destination. It will park itself with ease into tight parking spots. The chore of driving may not be there at all. But, one has to decide where to go, when to go and perhaps, how to go.

Drones may deliver packages for the courier companies. Couriering may get faster and individualized. Robots may replace workers in factories and servers in restaurants.

Novel Services

With the improvement in technology, the service needs of people increased in the recent couple of decades. In fact, service industry has become dominant. With more of technological advances in the not too distant future, people may see the possibility of and hence desire services that were not thought of hitherto. For example, it may sound bizarre today; but, many men and women may prefer a robot or a speaking computer/mobile for company.

Technology may fill some of their emotional needs. 'Emotional service' may be one kind of service. As it is, the mobile phone and so-called social media like Facebook and Twitter have replaced conversations between people from personal – physically next to each other – to a distant but 'connected' mode. Many such 'friendly' relationships can be expressed from a distance.

But, the Core of Operations Management Will Remain the Same

The core of operations management – the need for agility, time being the essence, the necessity for connectedness, the human element in management, the cost consciousness, the quest for excellence – is and will always stay. The outer cover viz. the infrastructure, the type of product and the variety of services may change.

Whether it is a robotic server or otherwise, the needs of the customer for a gastronomically appealing dish, cleanliness, timely service, efficient service, underlying courtesy, pleasing ambience and so on will always remain. If there were to be another similar restaurant, they would compete on the same basis.

A drone may deliver letters and packages. But, whatever the implement, the courier company's system of operations, its basic principles, its tracking needs and its desired end result will be the same.

> **Principle 21**
> **Welcome technological advances in operations. However, core essentials of POM remain the same.**

A robot companion may provide emotional service. It will be the case of a novel service product. Yet, the task of the manufacturer and the operations management to make an unfailing companion may require the same Six Sigma and TQM fundamentals; perhaps, the requirement may be even more stringent as emotions would be at stake.

Whatever service is desired, it has to be provided faultlessly, quickly, timely, effectively, productively, changeably and preferably at affordable cost. Machines have changed but not human beings. The basic principles governing his/her service delivery and, therefore, for operations, remain the same.

Technology will Lend Adaptability and Agility; and will Expect the Same in Return

When human input is replaced, in some parts of the operations, by a machine (thinking or otherwise), it may improve adaptability and agility of the service/making operations. By the same token, such a change may suppose that the replaced humans quickly learn another employable skill. Or else, they may become jobless. Think of automated driving and the loss of job for millions of drivers worldwide. If they have not acquired any other skill, they may join the ranks of the unemployed.

Similar things may happen with several other manufacturing and service industries. Many tasks – worker level, maintenance, clerical, office administration and secretarial – may now be replaced by technologies like Artificial Intelligence and the Internet of Things.

Already the world is facing the effects of automation. Automobiles and process industries have become so automated that they need a small fraction of the earlier manpower. Several workers have become unemployed. All over the USA and Europe, this phenomenon has spread a strong discontentment with political repercussions. Improved operations necessitate that people are agile and adapt to new kinds of jobs and services that will arise.

Principle 22
Always remember:
Technology can be a double-edged sword.
Use it;
with caution for now and posterity.

Pretty Devil of Operations

Beyond the 'producer and customer/consumer' and 'service provider and service receiver' there is a larger society. When an operation is run, it will have effects beyond the boundaries of the factory or the service facility. When mining operations are carried out, they have effects on the soil in and around the mine – many a times on the environment far and wide from the location of the operation. A thermal power plant using coal is considerably polluting. Same is true of other processing plants. Liquid effluents can spoil the water bodies – surface water and ground-water deep below the soil.

It is the production/service operations and their products that have the potential to do this damage. The technology of operations and its products is like a pretty devil. 'Pretty' till we deal with cautiously; else it could turn devilish.

The situation may sometimes reach a 'breakdown' point. Look at Delhi city's pollution woes. Or the smog of Beijing and Paris. The operations, therefore, have a responsibility to ensure that the environment is not affected because of them. Breakdown situations should not arise; these should be prevented by suitable actions. A production or service operation may cease to exist, but environmental impacts continue to exist much beyond. Every production or service operation should, therefore, be carried out with abundant precaution. There is an onerous responsibility to ensure that environmental and social considerations are never overlooked.

www.ingramcontent.com/pod-product-compliance
Ingram Content Group UK Ltd.
Pitfield, Milton Keynes, MK11 3LW, UK
UKHW021359190726
13845UKWH00028B/769

9 789386 643056